From the moment they met, Mommy could see,
That Waldo was special and brave as could be.
She loved his marking - a question mark flipped around!
See if you can spot it - go ahead, turn this book upside down!

Waldo the Wonder Dog is no normal-sized mutt,
He's long, extra fluffy, and has a really big butt.
He can hear very far and has a super strong nose.
Waldo can smell anything, even your stinky toes!

Waldo The Wonder Dog

A true story about a talented corgi who rescued his owner.

Author: Jess Parker
Illustrator: Maggie Tessier
Publisher: Connex Publishing

Dedication: To my amazing husband, Brady Parker.
While Waldo was the hero on the day of the rescue, you were the hero every day after. Thank you for taking care of me and our family with love and strength. And to our nephew & niece, Paxton & Paisley, I wrote this story with you in mind. May it bring you joy, spark your imagination, and remind you that even the smallest heroes can make a big difference.

This is an interactive storybook! Each section has a QR code that leads to videos of the real-life Waldo in action.

Waldo the Wonder Dog has always been a special pup.
From the day he came home, Mommy's heart lifted up.
She always wanted a furry best friend of her own,
And with Waldo beside her, she'll never be alone.

Did you know that corgis are a herding breed?
That's why they bark loud and run at top speed.
Waldo's legs may be little, but wow, can he fly!
Don't blink or you'll miss him soar through the sky!

Waldo the Wonder Dog is very smart.
He loves learning new tricks with all of his heart.
Mommy teaches Waldo all kinds of fun things.
Like play dead, roll over, he even sings!

He'll show off his moves, wave hello, or paw shakes,
If there's a big tasty treat, he'll do what it takes!
Waldo's clever and kind, always ready to play,
He might just become a hero one day...

Waldo the Wonder Dog loves making new friends.
Both doggos and humans, the fun never ends!
He easily makes pals wherever he goes,
Spreading joy, love, and laughter to those that he knows.

He visits every festival that he can find,
Showing off his big booty, he's one of a kind!
Wearing all sorts of costumes, Waldo puts on a show,
Spreading cheer with a wiggle and friendly hello!

Waldo the Wonder Dog volunteers around town,
He loves helping others turn a frown upside down.
Like giving out kisses, cheering those who are sad,
Waldo makes everything a little less bad.

Waldo's favorite way to let off some steam,
Is dipping his paws in a nice, cold stream!
Did you know that corgi bums float?
It's true, they do! Thanks to their fluffy fur coat!

Waldo the Wonder Dog is an internet star,
Sharing his message of love from near to far.
With silly doggy dances and playful tricks,
Waldo's videos quickly get thousands of clicks!

He's up for adventure, with joy as his guide.
No journey's too far, no dream is too wide.
He follows his Mommy wherever she goes,
Through sunshine and rain, or even in snow.

Waldo the Wonder Dog was put to the test,
When one morning walk turned into a quest.
Mommy slipped on the path, they both heard a crack,
She broke her leg—*Thump!*—landed flat on her back!

No phone to call home, she cried out for help.
Waldo had to do something, he started to yelp.
He kissed her face quick, then dashed off in haste,
He went to find help, there was no time to waste.

**Waldo the Wonder Dog knew just what to do,
His paws hit the ground, and away he flew.
He tugged on a pant leg, and barked "Come quick!"
He led them to Mommy and gave her a lick.**

Then he ran off again, without any delay,
And came back with more help to save the day.
This stubby pup now stood proud and tall,
Waldo saved the day from Mommy's big fall.

Waldo the Wonder Dog, a hero, it's true!
The story spread quickly, soon everyone knew.
Radio, TV, and magazines too,
All told the world what Waldo could do.

His rescue tale was shared with glee,
For this pup who showed true bravery.
They called him a hero for what he had done,
A fearless corgi, whose quest was won!

Waldo the Wonder Dog, loved by one and all,
His town threw a party at City Hall.
They gave him gifts and treats galore,
A hero like Waldo, they couldn't ignore.

Waldo made lots of friends in his moment of fame,
Everyone cheered and shouted his name.
They placed a hero's cape across his back,
But his favorite part? When they gave him a snack!

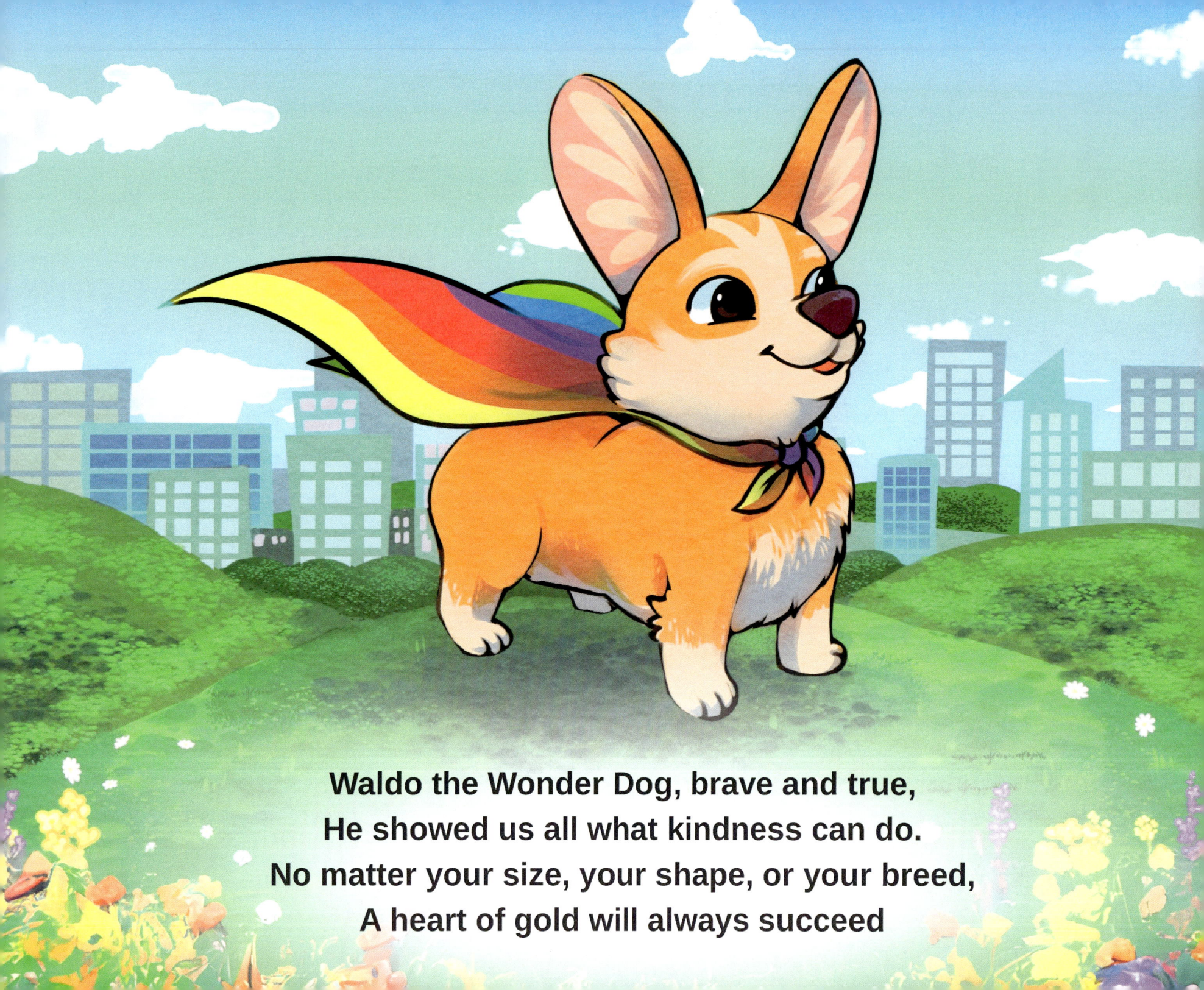

Waldo the Wonder Dog, brave and true,
He showed us all what kindness can do.
No matter your size, your shape, or your breed,
A heart of gold will always succeed

His story of love has touched every heart,
Mommy knew he was special right from the start.
He's proven how mighty a little corgi can be,
Who knows what this Wonder Dog's next mission will be!

Become A Waldo Warrior

Fun Fact: Waldo's fans are called Waldo Warriors - It's true!
And guess what? You could be one too!
If you stand for love and peace in all that you do,
There's a spot in Waldo's crew waiting for you!

Waldo likes to give back, because he's got a big heart,
And now's your chance to play a special part.
Give what you can to support the cause,
To help our furry friends with paws!

Did you know that 10% of proceeds from 'Waldo the Wonder Dog' are donated to The Humane Society of Canada? Thank you for helping us spread love, joy, and hope to animals in need. Want to make an even bigger impact? Scan the QR code to donate directly and keep the kindness going.

Waldo The Wonder Dog

Waldo The Wonder Dog

Written by Jess Parker

Copyright © 2025 Jess Parker

Published by Connex Publishing

Illustrated by Maggie Tessier

ISBN: 978-1-0693801-9-7

Printed in Canada

First Edition

All rights reserved. No portion of this book may be reproduced transmitted, downloaded or changed in any form or by any means whether electronic or mechanical without express written permission from the Author.

QR Codes: We make every effort to keep these QR codes active, but technology changes quickly, and we can't guarantee they will work forever.

For more information, go to: Waldothewonderdog.com

Waldo The Wonder Dog
Sticker Page

www.ingramcontent.com/pod-product-compliance
Lightning Source LLC
Chambersburg PA
CBRC100813010526
44119CB00046B/503